God creates the world.

Genesis 1:1—2:25

Adam and Eve disobey God.

Genesis 3:1-24

Noah builds an ark.

Genesis 6:1-22

God keeps Noah and the animals safe.
Genesis 7:1-24

God makes a promise. Genesis 8:1—9:17

Abram travels to a new home.

Genesis 12:1-9

Isaac is born.

Genesis 15:1-6; 17:1-8; 18:1-15; 21:1-7

Abraham's servant finds a wife for Isaac.
Genesis 24:1-67

Isaac chooses not to fight.

Genesis 26:12-33

Jacob tricks Esau.

Genesis 25:19-34; 27:1-41

Jacob has a dream.

Genesis 27:41-45; 28:10-22

Jacob goes home.

Genesis 31:1—33:20

Joseph's brothers sell him.

Genesis 37:2-36

Joseph helps Pharaoh.

Genesis 39:1—41:49

Joseph forgives his brothers.

Genesis 42:1—45:28

The people of Israel are slaves in Egypt.

Exodus 1:1-22

God protects baby Moses.

Exodus 2:1-10

God talks to Moses.

Exodus 3:1—4:17

Moses says,
"Let my
people go."

Exodus 5:1—12:32

Moses leads the people out of Egypt.

Exodus 12:33-39; 13:17-22

God makes a path through the Red Sea. Exodus 14:1-31

God gives manna to eat.

Exodus 16:1-36

God gives the Ten Commandments.

Exodus 19:1—24:18

The people bring gifts to make the Tabernacle.

Exodus 35:4—36:7

Moses sends twelve spies to the Promised Land.

Numbers 13:1—14:35

God provides water from a rock.

Numbers 20:1-13

Rahab helps two spies.

Joshua 2:1-24

The walls of Jericho fall down.

Joshua 6:1-27

Deborah helps Barak.

Judges 4:1—5:31

An angel talks to Gideon.

Judges 6:1-24

God helps Gideon defeat the Midianites.

Judges 7:1-21

Ruth shows love.
Ruth 1:1-22

Ruth helps Naomi.
Ruth 2:1—4:22

Samson is strong.

Judges 13:1-25; 16:1-22

God answers Hannah's prayer.

1 Samuel 1:1—2:11

**God speaks
to Samuel.**
1 Samuel 3:1-21

Samuel chooses a king.

1 Samuel 8:1—10:24

David plays his harp for King Saul.

1 Samuel 16:14-23

David fights Goliath.

1 Samuel 17:1-58

David and Jonathan are friends.

1 Samuel 18:1-4; 20:1-42

Abigail is wise.

1 Samuel 25:2-42

King Solomon is wise.
1 Kings 3:1-15

Solomon builds the Temple.

1 Kings 5:1—6:38; 7:13-51; 2 Chronicles 2:1—4:22

God sends ravens with food for Elijah.

1 Kings 17:1-6

**God answers
Elijah's prayer.**

1 Kings 18:16-39

Elijah goes to heaven.

2 Kings 2:1-14

Elisha helps a widow.

2 Kings 4:1-7

Naaman is healed.
2 Kings 5:1-19

Elisha leads a blind army.

2 Kings 6:8-23

Joash repairs the Temple.

2 Kings 12:1-15; 2 Chronicles 24:1-14

Hezekiah praises God.

2 Chronicles 30:1-27

Jonah disobeys God.

Jonah 1:1—2:10

Jonah preaches in Nineveh.
Jonah 3:1-10

Josiah hears God's Word.

2 Kings 22:1—23:3; 2 Chronicles 34:14-32

The king destroys the scroll of God's Words.

Jeremiah 36:1-32

Daniel and his friends choose to obey God.

Daniel 1:1-21

**God protects
Daniel's friends
in a furnace.**

Daniel 3:1-30

God protects Daniel in a den of lions. Daniel 6:1-28

Esther is chosen queen.
Esther 2:1-18

**Queen Esther
saves her people.**

Esther 4:1—7:10

Nehemiah rebuilds the walls.

Nehemiah 2:11—4:23

**An angel
visits Mary.**
Luke 1:26-38

Jesus is born.
Luke 2:1-7

Angels tell the good news of Jesus' birth to shepherds.

Luke 2:8-20

Wise men come to worship.
Matthew 2:1-12

Jesus escapes to Egypt.

Matthew 2:13-23

Mary and Joseph look for Jesus.

Luke 2:41-52

John the Baptist preaches about the coming Savior.
Matthew 3:1-12; Mark 1:1-8; Luke 3:1-20

John baptizes Jesus.

Matthew 3:13-17; Mark 1:9-11;
Luke 3:21,22; John 1:29-34

When Jesus is tempted, He obeys God's Word.

Matthew 4:1-11; Mark 1:12,13; Luke 4:1-13

Jesus says, "Follow me."

Matthew 4:18-22; Mark 1:16-20; Luke 5:1-11; John 1:40-42

Jesus heals Peter's mother-in-law.

Matthew 8:14,15;
Mark 1:29-31;
Luke 4:38,39

Jesus talks to Nicodemus about God's love.

John 3:1-21

Jesus talks to a Samaritan woman.

John 4:1-42

Jesus calms a storm.
Matthew 8:23-27; Mark 4:35-41;
Luke 8:22-25

Jesus heals a paralyzed man.

Matthew 9:2-8; Mark 2:1-12; Luke 5:17-26

A woman touches Jesus and is healed.

Matthew 9:20-22; Mark 5:25-34; Luke 8:43-48

Jesus heals Jairus's daughter.
Matthew 9:18-26; Mark 5:22-43; Luke 8:40-56

Jesus uses a boy's lunch to feed 5,000 people.

Matthew 14:13-21; Mark 6:30-44; Luke 9:10-17; John 6:1-15

Jesus walks on the water and helps His friends.

Matthew 14:22-33; Mark 6:45-52; John 6:16-21

Jesus heals a man who couldn't hear or talk.

Mark 7:31-37

Only one man says thank you to Jesus.
Luke 17:11-19

Jesus loves the children.

Matthew 19:13-15; Mark 10:13-16; Luke 18:15-17

Jesus helps a blind man see.

John 9:1-41

Jesus tells about a good Samaritan.

Luke 10:25-37

Mary listens to Jesus.
Luke 10:38-42

Jesus tells about a patient father.

Luke 15:11-32

Zaccheus climbs
a tree to see Jesus.
Luke 19:1-9

Jesus brings Lazarus back to life.

John 11:1-44

The people welcome Jesus to Jerusalem.
Matthew 21:1-11; Mark 11:1-11; Luke 19:28-44

Jesus clears the Temple.

Matthew 21:12-16; Mark 11:12-19; Luke 19:45-48

A poor woman gives all she has.

Mark 12:41-44; Luke 21:1-4

A woman shows love to Jesus.
Matthew 26:6-13; Mark 14:3-9; John 12:2-8

Jesus washes His friends' feet.

John 13:1-17

Jesus eats a special meal with His friends.

Matthew 26:17-30; Mark 14:12-26; Luke 22:7-38

Peter lies about knowing Jesus.

Matthew 26:69-75; Mark 14:66-72;
Luke 22:55-62; John 18:15-18,25-27

Jesus dies on the cross.

Matthew 27:32-56; Mark 15:21-41;
Luke 23:26-49; John 19:17-37

Jesus talks to Mary in the garden.
John 20:10-18

My Bible Coloring Book • 99

Jesus talks to His friends.

Mark 16:14; Luke 24:36-43; John 20:19-23

Thomas believes when he sees Jesus.

John 20:24-29

Jesus cooks breakfast on the beach.

John 21:1-25

Jesus goes back to heaven.

Luke 24:50-53; Acts 1:1-11

God sends the Holy Spirit.
Acts 2:1-13

Barnabas shows his love for Jesus by sharing.

Acts 4:32-37

Philip tells the good news about Jesus to an Ethiopian man.

Acts 8:26-40

Jesus talks to Saul.

Acts 9:1-19

Saul escapes in a basket. Acts 9:19-25

God brings Dorcas to life again after Peter prays.
Acts 9:32-43

Peter preaches to Cornelius.

Acts 10:1-48

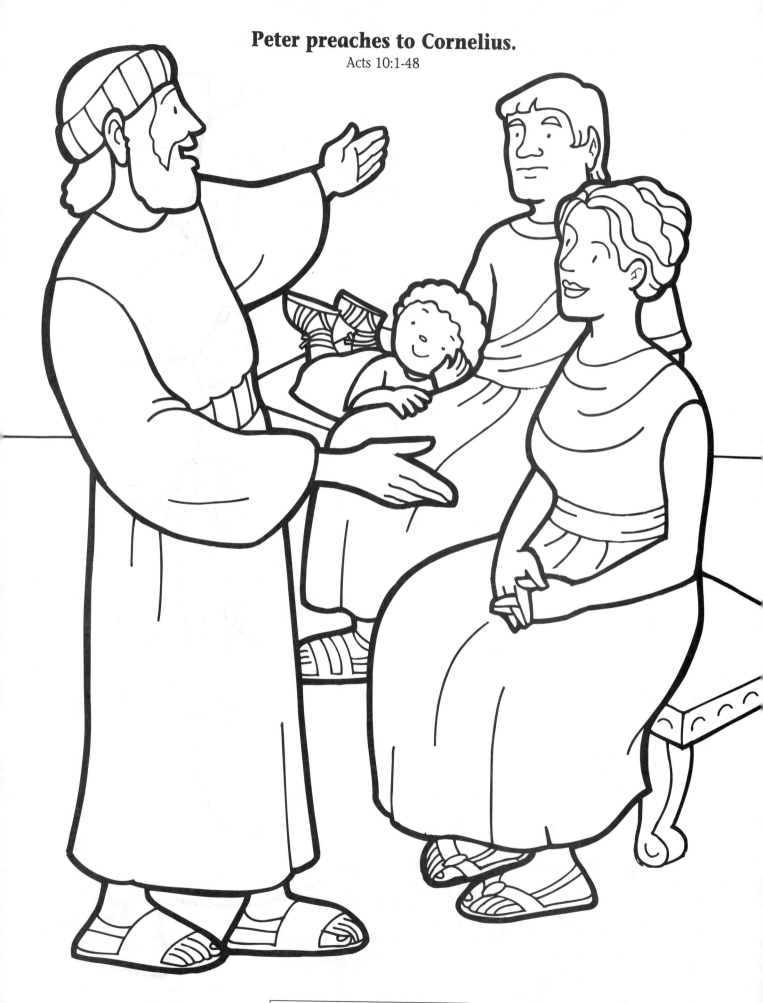

An angel frees Peter.

Acts 12:1-19

Lydia believes in Jesus.

Acts 16:11-15

Paul and Silas sing praise to God in jail.

Acts 16:16-40

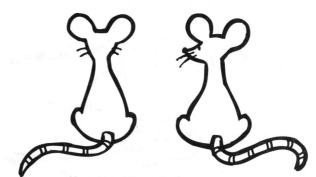

Paul tells a king about Jesus.
Acts 25:13—26:32

Paul's ship wrecks in a storm.
Acts 27:1-44

A snake bites Paul.
Acts 28:1-6

Paul writes letters to help others follow Jesus.

2 Timothy 1:1—4:22

Paul sends Onesimus home.

Philemon 1-25

John writes good news.

Revelation 1:1,2,9-11; 21:3-5

Dear God,

Thank You for loving us. Thank You for giving us the Bible so we can learn about Your love. Thank You for Your plan to show love to everyone all over the world. We are glad You love us so much that You sent Jesus. Please help us to learn more about You and to trust You more.

In Jesus' name, amen.